W9-DDR-896

Fab FASHIONS
You Can Make and Share

by Mari Bolte
illustrated by Paula Franco

CAPSTONE PRESS
a capstone imprint

Table of Contents

Pack your bags for fun with the Sleepover Girls!
Every Friday, Maren, Ashley, Delaney, and Willow get
together for crafts, fashion, cooking, and, of course,
girl talk! Read the books, get to know the girls,
and dive in to this book of cool projects that are
Sleepover Girl staples!

Create a charm bracelet that represents you
and your besties, or turn an everyday skirt into a
trail of tulle. Let your dog have its day by creating
a cute collar, or wear your love for Hollywood
hotties (Luke Lewis, anyone?) on your sleeve. Grab
some glue, phone some friends, and start crafting
with your very own Sleepover Girls.

MEET THE SLEEPOVER GIRLS!

Willow Marie Keys

Patient and kind, Willow is a wonderful confidante and friend. (Just ask her twin, Winston!) She is also a budding artist with creativity for miles. Willow's Bohemian style suits her flower child within.

Maren Melissa Taylor

Maren is what you'd call "personality-plus"—sassy, bursting with energy, and always ready with a sharp one-liner. You'll often catch Maren wearing a hoodie over a sports tee and jeans. An only child, Maren has adopted her friends as sisters.

Ashley Francesca Maggio

Ashley is the baby of a lively Italian family. This fashionista-turned-blogger is on top of every style trend via her blog, Magstar. Vivacious and mischievous, Ashley is rarely sighted without her beloved "purse puppy," Coco.

Delaney Ann Brand

Delaney's smart, motivated, and always on the go! You'll usually spot low-maintenance Delaney in a ponytail and jeans (and don't forget her special charm bracelet, with charms to symbolize her Sleepover Girl buddies.)

Record Label Jingles

Ashley knew Sophie was her style soul mate when Sophie first walked into homeroom. Of course the daughter of a record label bigwig would dress like a rock star! Match Sophie's Hollywood look by making your own guitar pick earrings.

WHAT YOU'LL NEED

small hole punch

guitar picks

small jump rings

beads

needlenose pliers

surgical steel earring wires

1 Use the hole punch to create holes at the top and bottom of each guitar pick.

2 Thread a jump ring through the charm's top hole.

3 Attach guitar pick to the earring loops.

4 Twist the wire to fasten. Close jump ring.

5 Continue adding picks by using more jump rings. Add beads to accent the picks, if desired.

6 Repeat steps 2–5 to make a second earring.

Phone a Friend

There are hundreds of options for covering your cell, but which one is you? Personalize your device and start talking and texting with style.

WHAT YOU'LL NEED

clear cell phone cover (with or without silver bumper)

pencil

sparkly scrapbook paper

letter stencil

black permanent marker

pink permanent marker

craft glue

flat-backed jewel

1 Remove the cardboard insert from the inside of the cell phone cover. Trace the insert onto the back of the scrapbook paper. (If your your cover doesn't have an insert, trace the cover instead.)

2 Lay the scrapbook paper inside the cell phone cover, with the sparkly side facing out.

3 Lay the stencil over the back of the cover. Carefully use the permanent markers to trace the stencil's pattern onto the cell phone cover.

4 Remove the stencil, and touch up any parts that may need it. Use markers to add additional decoration as desired.

5 Glue the jewel onto the cell phone case. Let dry completely before using.

TIP:
Do not glue the scrapbook paper to the cell phone cover. Instead, trace the insert on other paper patterns, and switch them out whenever you need a change.

A Map Made in Heaven

Willow's the artsy one in the group. With a little paper mache and a stack of old maps, you can be too!

WHAT YOU'LL NEED

necklace clasp

6 feet (1.8 meters) of elastic necklace cord

old maps

glue stick

wooden skewers

clear acrylic gloss coating sealant

30 to 40 .25-inch (.6-centimeter) or larger beads

seed beads

1 Tie one end of the cord to one part of the necklace clasp.

2 Cut 24 triangles from the map. Each triangle should be 10 inches (25.4 cm) long and 1 inch (2.5 cm) wide on one side.

3 Cut 24 more triangles from the map. Each triangle should be 10 inches long and .5 inch (1.3 cm) wide on each side.

4 Put one triangle on your workspace, pattern side down. Rub glue on the triangle.

5 Put a skewer on the wide edge of the triangle. Roll the paper tightly around the stick. Glue down the tip, and slide the bead off the skewer. Repeat to create a total of 48 paper beads.

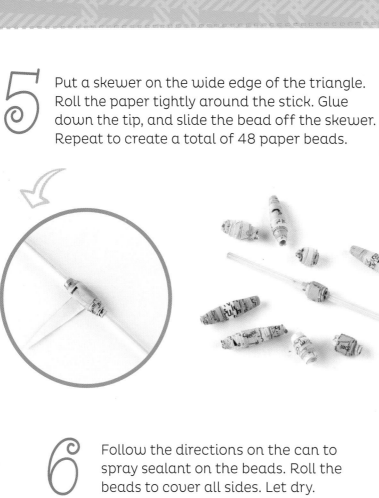

6 Follow the directions on the can to spray sealant on the beads. Roll the beads to cover all sides. Let dry.

7 While the beads are drying, plan your necklace's pattern. Lay out beads in the order they will be strung.

8   When the rolled beads are dry, begin threading them onto the cord.

9   Continue threading until the necklace is the length you want.

10   Tie the cord to the other half of the necklace clasp. Cut off the extra cord. Depending on how long you want the necklace, you might not use all the beads or you might need more.

Follow Frisco!

Delaney's dog, Frisco, loves going on walks. A good leash is an important accessory for any dog lover. Make sure your dog's accessories are as fashionable as yours!

WHAT YOU'LL NEED

leash clip

one strand gray paracord, 5 feet, 5 inches (1.7 m) long

one strand pink paracord, 5 feet, 5 inches long

1. Snap the leash clip to a secure surface (or use tape or a clamp.)

2. Thread the paracord through the ring of the snap. You should have four even strands of paracord.

3. Starting braiding by crossing the strand on the right over the two center strands.

4. Cross the strand on the left over the two center strands. Knot the two crossed strands together.

5. Repeat steps 3–4 with the other two strands. Continue alternating strand pairs until almost all the leash has been braided.

6. Tie a knot 5 inches (12.7 cm) from the end of the paracord.

7. Braid the remaining 5 inches of paracord. Then loop, and tie the ends.

Best-Dressed Pooch

Walk the runway with the Sleepover Girls and Valley View Pet Rescue in high style! Your pooch will be the star of the fashion show with this dapper bow-wow bow tie.

WHAT YOU'LL NEED

3 inch by 6 inch (7.6 by 15.2 cm) piece of fabric

iron

needle and thread

2 inch by 3 inch (5 cm by 7.6 cm) piece of fabric

1-inch (2.5 cm-) wide Velcro strip

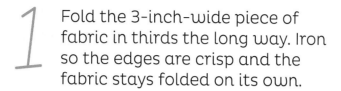

1 Fold the 3-inch-wide piece of fabric in thirds the long way. Iron so the edges are crisp and the fabric stays folded on its own.

2 Fold the short ends of the fabric so they meet in the center. Iron the folds.

3 Sew a running stitch through the center of the fabric. Then pull the thread. This should pull the fabric into a bow shape. Set aside.

4 Repeat step 1 with the 2-inch-wide piece of fabric.

5 Wrap the strip of fabric around the center of the bow. Stitch into place.

6 Sew the Velcro strip to the back of the tie. Use it to attach the tie to your dog's collar.

Friends Are Charming

Delaney has a bracelet with charms that represent each of her friends. Artsy Willow's charm is a paint palette. Actress Maren is a drama mask. Kissy lips represent Ashley. And Delany's charm is a dog bone! Find special charms that represent your friends. Then create your own charming charm bracelet.

WHAT YOU'LL NEED

section of large-link chain long enough to fit around your wrist

6 to 8 charms

12 to 20 1-inch (2.5-cm) head pins

variety of beads

round-nose pliers

bent-nose pliers

12 to 20 8-millimeter jump rings

1 10-mm jump ring

lobster claw clasp

1 Lay the chain flat on your work surface. Place the head pins and charms along its length, planning how many charms you want to use. Keep in mind when the head pins get beaded, they'll take up extra space.

2 Thread beads onto each head pin, leaving ¼ to ⅓ inch (.6 to .8 cm) of wire at the top.

3 Loop the top of each head pin closed with the round-nosed pliers.

4 Use the bent-nose pliers to attach each head pin to a small jump ring. Then attach the jump ring to the chain. Repeat until all charms are attached.

5 Attach the 10-mm jump ring to the last link on one end of the chain.

6 Thread an 8-mm jump ring through the small loop on the lobster claw clasp. Attach the jump ring to the last link on the other end of the chain.

Hair Flair

A few extra minutes can mean the difference between post-sleepover bedhead and sophisticated style. All you need for these easy updos is a curling iron, bobby pins, and a hair clip.

OFF THE FACE

1 Use a curling iron or hot rollers to create long, loose waves all over your head.

2 Gather hair from the sides and the top. Pull hair into a half-ponytail. Secure hair with a clip or a barrette rather than a ponytail holder.

3 Fan out the hair by loosening pieces from the clip. If you'd like, you can even pull a few pieces loose to create ringlets in front.

SIMPLE FRENCH TWIST

1 Gather all of your hair in a low ponytail near the top of your neck. Hold the hair in your hand rather than securing with a ponytail holder.

2 Twist and lift the hair upward. Continue twisting until you've reached the end of the hair.

3 Hold the twist in place near the top of your head. Tuck the excess top hair underneath the existing twist. Use bobby pins to hold the twist in place.

Bracelets for Your *Besties*

Making matching bracelets for all your Sleepover Girls is quick and easy. A pack of rubber bands is all you need to create a pile of stretchy fun.

1 Use your fingers to press a rubber band into a flat, oval shape. Thread a c-clip onto the band.

2 Pull the rubber band over two fingers, twisting in the center. Make sure the clip is between your fingers.

3 Pull a rubber band over your fingers, but do not twist.

4 Pull another rubber band over your fingers, but do not twist.

5 Pull the bottom band up and over one of your fingers. Repeat with the other side.

6 Repeat steps 2–5 (without adding more c-clips) until the bracelet is the desired length.

7 To finish the bracelet, add two extra rubber bands. Then slip the bracelet off your fingers. Remove the extra bands. This should create loops that you can pull over the c-clip.

Magstar Style

Ashley's fashion blog, Magstar, is the cutting edge of style. Show your love by wearing the Magstar logo around town.

WHAT YOU'LL NEED

computer printer

freezer paper

pink felt

iron

craft knife or scissors

glitter glue

light blue felt

craft glue

hair clip

1 Set up the printer so the ink will print onto the matte side of the freezer paper.

Decide on a font for the letter. When you have picked one out, print it out onto the freezer paper.

 Cut out the letter and decide how you want it placed on the pink felt.

Iron the freezer paper onto the felt, using the wool setting. This should take about 30 seconds.

Use a craft knife or scissors to cut away any extra paper around the letter. Then use the knife to cut out the letter.

 Trace the letter shape with glitter glue. Let dry.

 Cut out a star shape from the light blue felt.

 Glue the letter to the star. Let dry.

 Use glue to attach the logo to the top of the hair clip.

Sweet Dreams

Get the best night's sleep ever with a special slumber party pillow. The classic fleece tie pillow gets an update with bright colors, tidy knots, and a shape that all Sleepover Girls will love.

WHAT YOU'LL NEED

two 1 yard (.9 meters)
square pieces of fleece,
in different colors

scissors

ruler

chalk

fiberfill

1 Cut two heart shapes out of the fleece. Make them as large and as even as possible.

2 On one piece of fabric, use the ruler and chalk to draw a smaller heart 4 inches (10 cm) from the edge of the fabric. Make a mark every inch around the chalk heart. Then draw fringe lines that extend to the edge of the fabric.

3 Stack the fabric hearts on top of each other. Cut the fringe lines, through both layers of fleece.

4 Fold the fringe toward the center of the heart. Make a small vertical cut in the center of both pieces of fleece.

5 Push both pieces of fringe through the cut. Pull the fringe completely through. Continue until almost all the fringe has been pulled through.

6 Stuff the fleece with fiberfill. Then finish pulling the fringe, to seal the edges.

TIP:
To turn this pillow into a pet bed, use a larger piece of fleece. Stuff the pillow with old T-shirts or other fabric scraps.

I <3 Luke Lewis!

Maren loves singer Luke Lewis, and isn't afraid to show it. Wear your heart on your sleeve (literally!) with a homemade batik design.

WHAT YOU'LL NEED

white T-shirt
newspapers
pencil
blue gel school glue
acrylic craft paint
paintbrush

1. Lay the T-shirt flat on a newspaper-covered work surface. Place another layer of newspaper inside the shirt.

2. Lightly pencil your design onto the T-shirt.

3. Use the glue to draw over the design. Let dry completely, at least several hours or overnight.

4. Mix craft paint with water until the paint is completely thinned.

5. Paint over the design, using as many paint colors as desired. Let dry completely before flipping the shirt over to paint the back.

6. Soak the T-shirt in very warm water in a sink or bathtub for 30 minutes. This will loosen the glue.

7. Wring out the T-shirt and hang dry or dry in a machine.

Twirling In Tulle

Ashley and Sophie have an eye for fashion! These super shoppers zeroed in on a trendy tulle skirt that was the perfect combo of girly-meets-goth. Sew your own to suit your style with this twirling tulle tutu.

WHAT YOU'LL NEED

16 yards (14.6 m) of tulle; total amount will depend on your waist size and desired skirt length

needle and thread

skirt

ribbon

pins

Fold the tulle in half. Fold in half again.

At the top corner, cut a quarter-circle that equals the radius of your waist.

 Starting at the edge of the waist circle, add your desired skirt length to both the top and side edges of the fabric square. Make sure your desired length is slightly longer than your skirt. Cut out. You should now have a circle of fabric, with a hole in the middle.

 Repeat steps 1-3 until you have six circles of tulle.

 Stack and pin the layers of tulle, and loosely stitch them together at the waist. If the tulle is a little larger than your waist, pull the ends of the thread to scrunch the tulle.

 Sew the tulle to your skirt.

 Use a piece of ribbon or a belt to wear over the skirt. This will hide any seams, and give your skirt a finished look.

TIP:
To find your waist radius, measure your waist in inches. Then divide that number by 6.28.

SEWING BY HAND

Slide the thread through the eye of the needle. Tie the end of the thread into a knot. Poke the needle through the underside of the fabric. Pull the thread through the fabric to the knotted end. Poke your needle back through the fabric and up again to make a stitch.

Continue weaving the needle in and out of the fabric, making small stitches in a straight line. When you are finished sewing, make a loose stitch. Thread the needle through the loop and pull tight. Cut off remaining thread.

Read More

Doherty, Tricia. *Locker Looks and Study Nooks: A Crafting and Idea Book for a Smart Girl's Guide: Middle School.* American Girl. Middleton, Wisc.: American Girl, 2014.

Mattel. *Ever After High: Sleepover Spellebration Party Planner.* Ever After High. New York: Little, Brown and Co., 2014.

Kenney, Karen Latchana. *Cool Slumber Parties: Perfect Party Planning for Kids.* Minneapolis: ABDO Pub., 2012.

Snap Books are published by Capstone Press, 1710 Roe Crest Drive, North Mankato, Minnesota 56003

www.capstonepub.com

Library of Congress Cataloging-in-Publication Data
Bolte, Mari., author.
Fab fashions you can make and share / by Mari Bolte
illustrated by Paula Franco.
pages cm. — (Snap books. Sleepover girls crafts)
Summary: "Step-by-step instructions teach readers how to create clothing and accessories, including bags, jewelry, shirts, and skirts"—Provided by publisher.

ISBN 978-1-4914-1735-5 (library binding)
ISBN 978-1-4914-1740-9 (eBook PDF)

1. Dress accessories—Juvenile literature. 2. Handicraft—Juvenile literature. I. Franco, Paula, illustrator. II. Title.

TT649.8.B65 2015

646.3—dc23   2014012713

Designer: Tracy Davies McCabe
Craft Project Creator:
Kim Braun & Marcy Morin
Photo Stylist: Sarah Schuette
Art Director: Nathan Gassman
Production Specialist: Laura Manthe

Photo Credits:
All Photos By Capstone Press:
Karon Dubke

Artistic Effects:
shutterstock

Printed in the United States
of America in
North, Mankato, Minnesota.
032014   008087CGF14